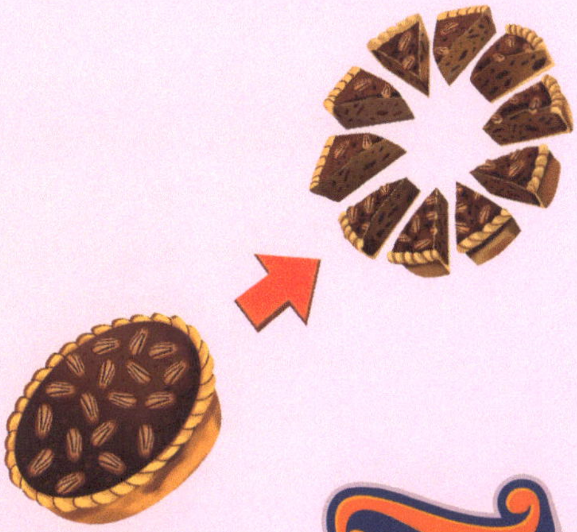

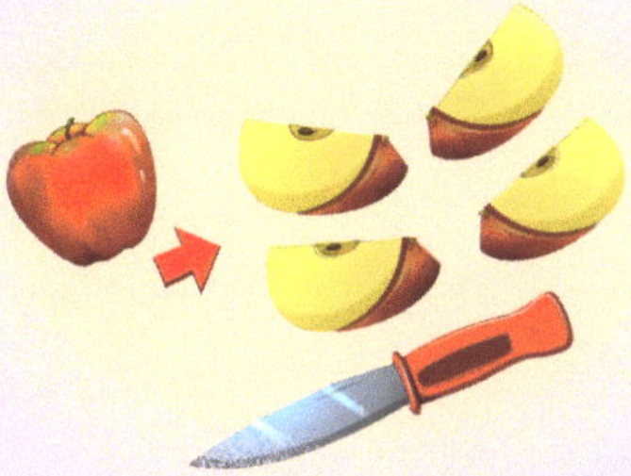

A Taste of Fractions

By Reigneer Nabong

Illustrations by
Blueberry Illustrations

Copyright © 2022 by Reigneer Nabong

All rights reserved.
No part of this book may be reproduced
or transmitted in any form or by any means
without written permission from the author.

ISBN-9798842955497

Dedication

This book about fractions is fittingly dedicated to my better "half," Melissa.

Thank you for your unwavering support and constant encouragement.

not cut in
any pieces

$\dfrac{1}{1}$

Donnie has 1 whole plum

If Donnie has a whole plum, $\dfrac{1}{1}$

he will have 1 piece out of 1 total piece.

1 ⟵ Number of piece Donnie has

1 ⟵ Number of total piece

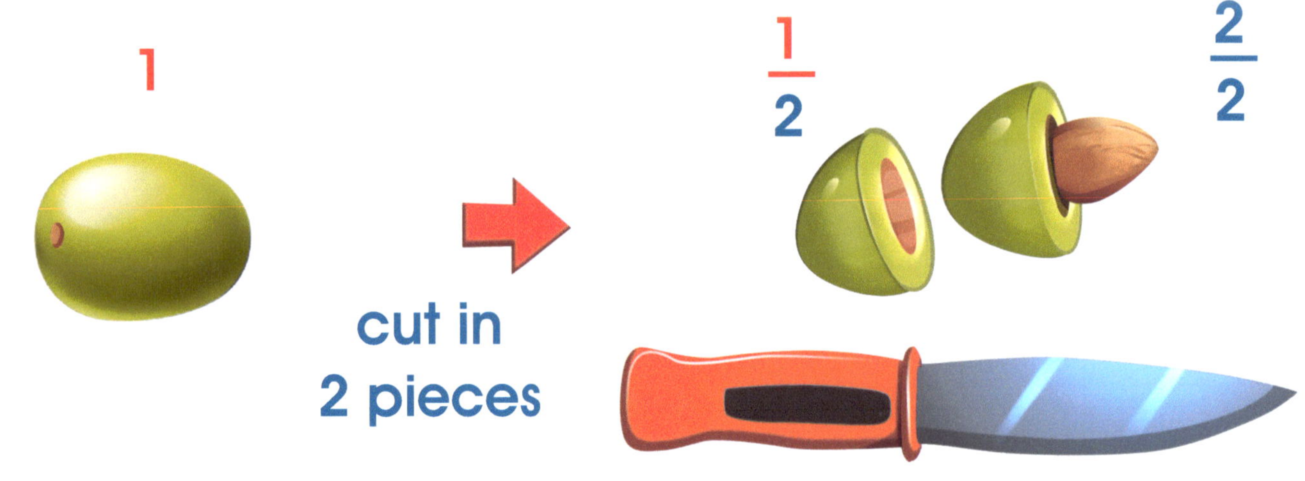

1
1
2
2
2
cut in
2 pieces
1
2 
Ms. Sally has 1 out of
total 2 pieces

If Ms. Sally cuts an olive in two pieces, $\frac{2}{2}$ and she takes 1 piece,

she will have $\frac{1}{2}$ or one-half,

1 piece out of 2 total pieces.

1 ←—— Number of piece Ms. Sally has

2 ←—— Number of total pieces

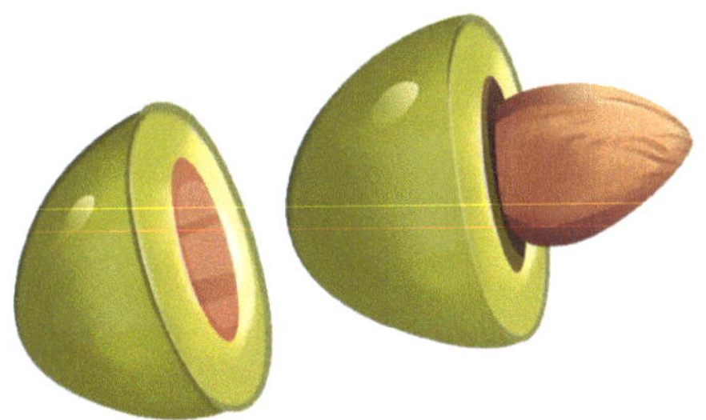

1
1
3
2
3
3
3
cut in
3 pieces

1
3
Lynn has 1 out of
total 3 pieces

If Lynn cuts a carrot in three pieces, $\frac{3}{3}$
and she takes 2 pieces,

she will have $\frac{2}{3}$ or two-thirds,

2 pieces out of 3 total pieces.

2 ⟵ Number of piece Lynn has

3 ⟵ Number of total pieces

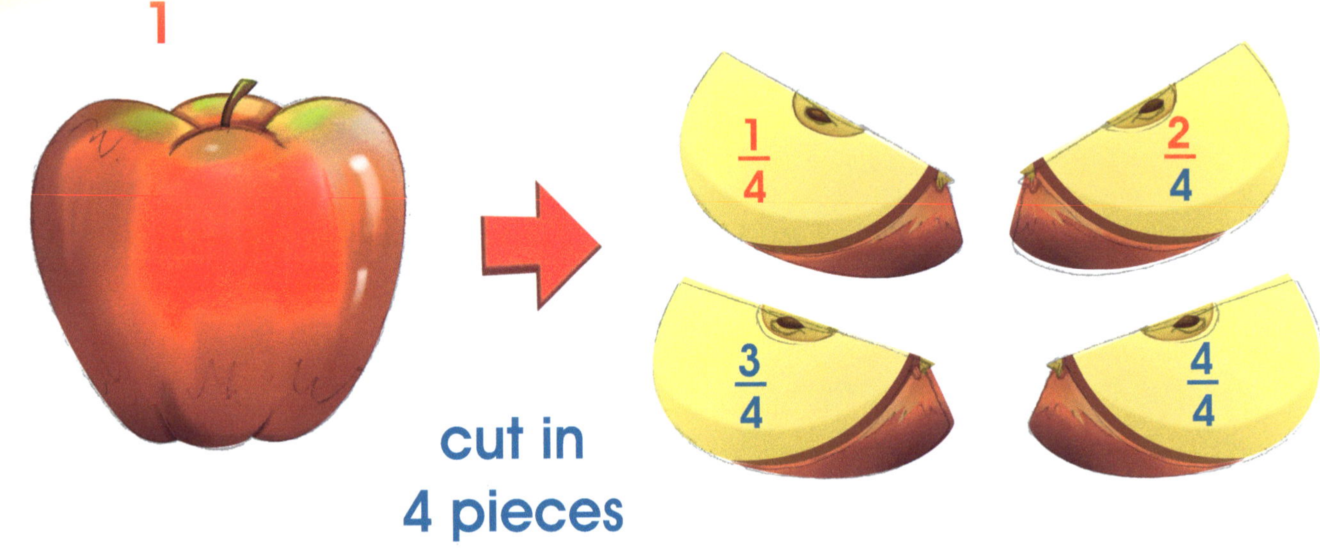

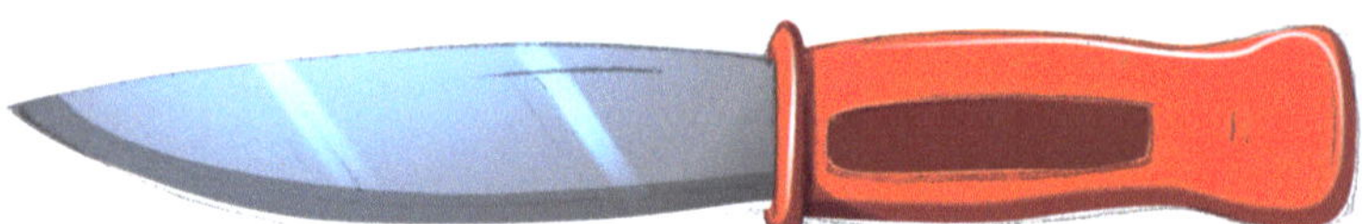

**Claire has 1 out of
total 4 pieces**

If Claire cuts an apple in four pieces, $\frac{4}{4}$ and she takes 2 pieces, she will have $\frac{2}{4}$ or two-fourths, 2 pieces out of 4 total pieces.

2 ⟵ Number of piece Claire has

4 ⟵ Number of total pieces

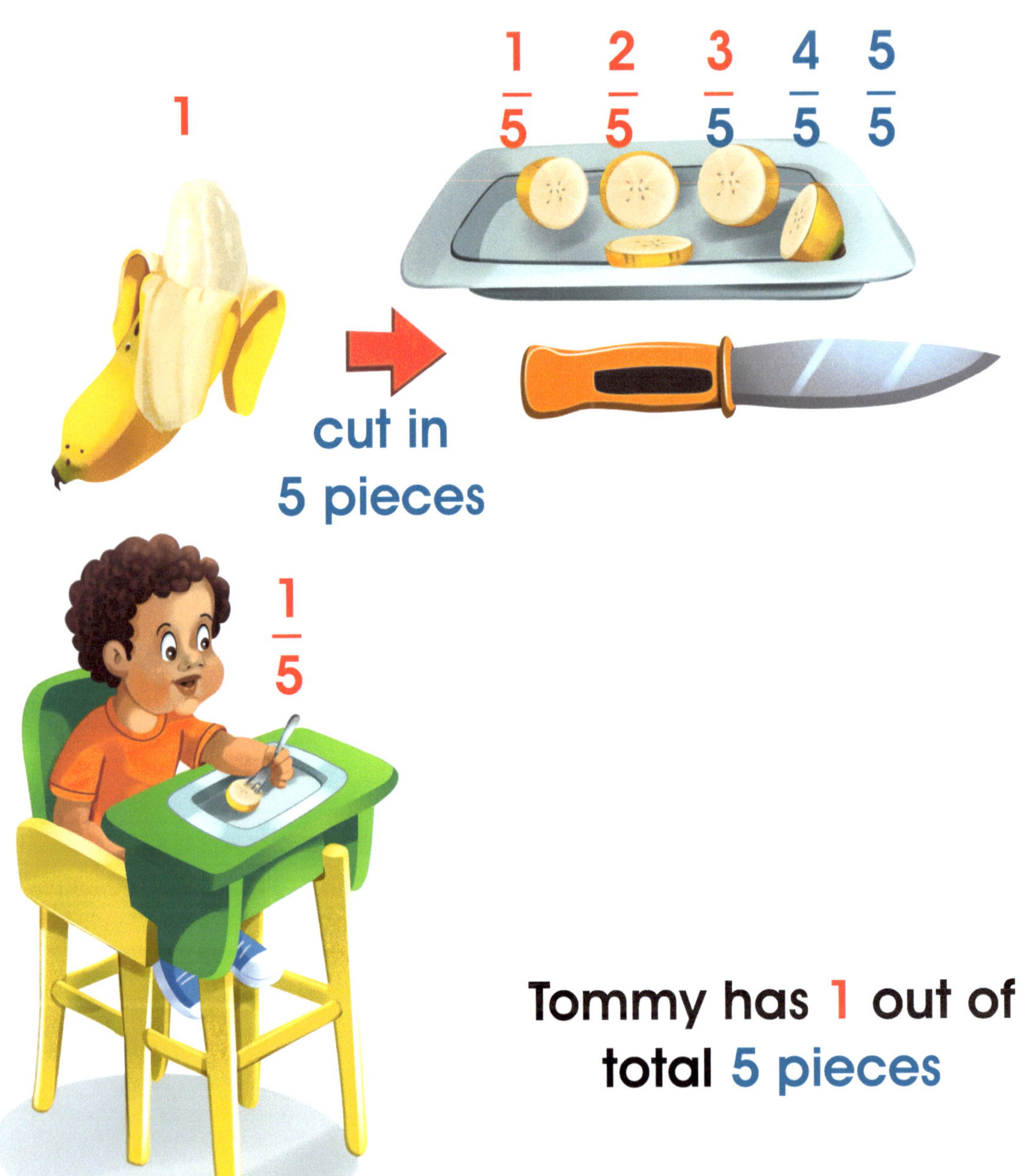

1
cut in
5 pieces
1/5
1/5 2/5 3/5 4/5 5/5
Tommy has 1 out of total 5 pieces

If Tommy cuts a banana in five pieces, $\frac{5}{5}$ and he takes 3 pieces,

he will have $\frac{3}{5}$ or three-fifths,

3 pieces out of 5 total pieces.

3 ⟵ Number of pieces Tommy has

5 ⟵ Number of total pieces

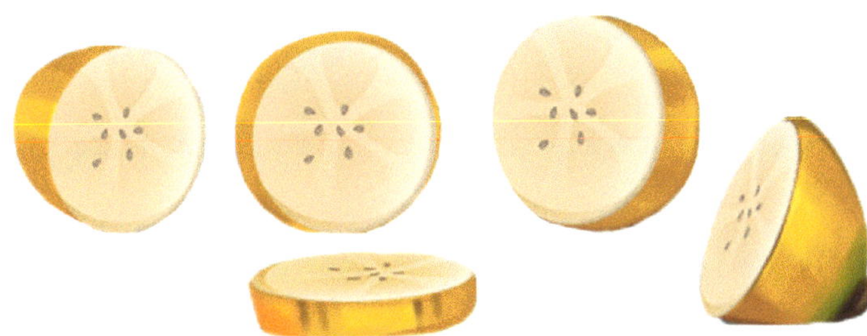

1
cut in
6 pieces
1/6 2/6 3/6 4/6 5/6
1/6
Mr. George has 1 out
of total 6 pieces

If Mr. George cuts a yam in six pieces, $\frac{6}{6}$ and he takes 3 pieces,

he will have $\frac{3}{6}$ or three-sixths,

3 pieces out of 6 total pieces.

3 ⟵ Number of pieces Mr. George has

6 ⟵ Number of total pieces

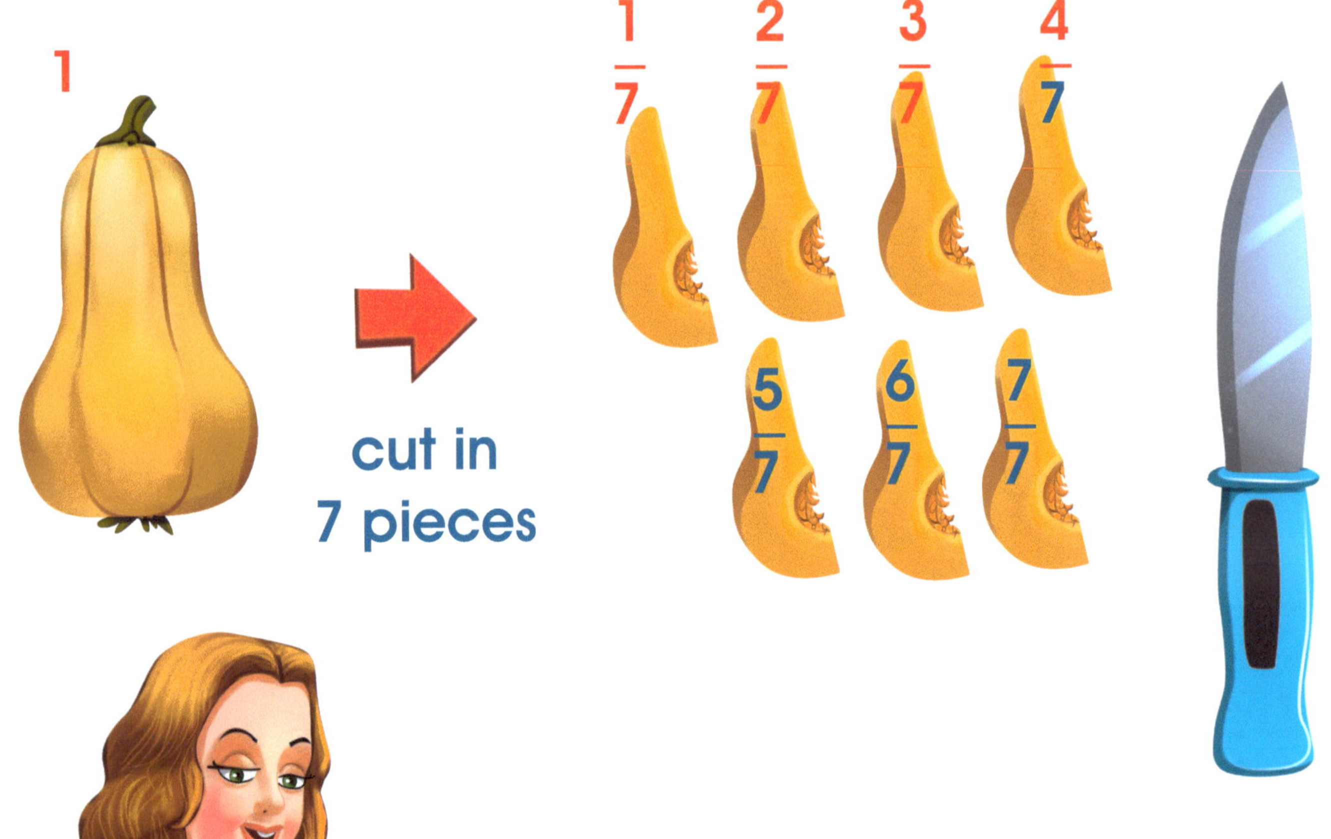

1
cut in
7 pieces
1/7
2/7
3/7
4/7
5/7
6/7
7/7
1/7
Ms. Nancy has 1 out of total 7 pieces

If Ms. Nancy cuts a squash in seven pieces, $\frac{7}{7}$ and she takes 4 pieces,

she will have $\frac{4}{7}$ or four-sevenths,

4 pieces out of 7 total pieces.

4 ⟵ Number of pieces Ms. Nancy has

7 ⟵ Number of total pieces

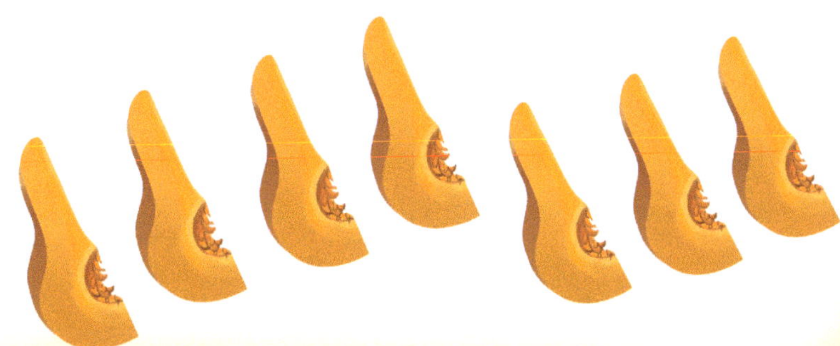

Brenda has 1 out of total 8 pieces

If Brenda cuts a pickle in eight pieces, $\dfrac{8}{8}$ and she takes 4 pieces,

she will have $\dfrac{4}{8}$ or four-eighths,

4 pieces out of 8 total pieces.

4 ⟵ Number of pieces Brenda has

8 ⟵ Number of total pieces

1

cut in
9 pieces

$\frac{1}{9}$ $\frac{2}{9}$ $\frac{3}{9}$

$\frac{4}{9}$ $\frac{5}{9}$ $\frac{6}{9}$

$\frac{7}{9}$ $\frac{8}{9}$ $\frac{9}{9}$

$\frac{1}{9}$

Alice has 1 out of total
9 pieces

If Alice cuts a watermelon in nine pieces, $\dfrac{9}{9}$ and she takes 5 pieces,

she will have $\dfrac{5}{9}$ or five-ninths,

5 pieces out of 9 total pieces.

5 ⟵ Number of pieces Alice has

9 ⟵ Number of total pieces

Kyle has **1** out of total
10 pieces

If Kyle cuts a pie in ten pieces, $\dfrac{10}{10}$ and he takes 5 pieces,

Kyle will have $\dfrac{5}{10}$ or five-tenths,

5 pieces out of 10 total pieces.

5 ⟵ Number of pieces Kyle has

10 ⟵ Number of total pieces

About the Author

The author has been an Information Technology professional for more than 30 years. He enjoys reading about new advancements in technology and how they can be used to improve our lives. He and his wife of fifteen years have four children ages 2 through 14: Keeks, Boots, Preets, and Paps. Their inquisitive nature has inspired the author to write educational books for young children

www.ingramcontent.com/pod-product-compliance
Lightning Source LLC
Chambersburg PA
CBHW042129110726
48006CB00003B/815